TOSSA
DE MAR

© POSTALES INTERNACIONAL COLOR, S.L. 2006

Encarnación, 180 bajos 1ª - 08025 BARCELONA

Tel. + Fax: 93 436 92 21

Photographs: "Archivo PIC"

2006 Edition

ISBN: 84-87587-55-0

D.Legal:B.3672-2006

Printed in Barcelona-Spain

Serper, S.L. - Ctra. de l'Hospitalet,22 - 08940 Cornellà (Barcelona)

INTRODUCTION

"Tossa flower of the sea", "Tossa pretty", "Tossa blue paradise", are the amorous compliments a poet, a musician and a painter have told her. An endless story if we try to collect all the compliments that artists have told it, inspired by the beautiful attractive of its landscape, its light, its grace.

Tossa has always awakened an unexplainable seduction in all those who have visited it and even more if they have met people o fan acute art sensitivity.

A long time ago, at the end of the 19th Century and the beginnings of the 20th, when in order to arrive to Tossa the traveller had to live a kina of adventure because of the difficult access to the city, Catalonian painters and landscape painters began to visit it. They discovered, hidden in its valley, a village that kept, with slight foreign influences, the pass of the centuries over its houses and walls covered with dazzling lime the firsts and of ancient mosses the honourable medieval ruins. For these artists, landscape was a continuous surprise but also a torture and a joy, in their try to show it in their canvases. It

would take long naming all of them but we can make reference, amongst the first, to Roig and Soler, Brull, Barrau, Mir, Masriera, etc. Tossa's name became international. In a lot of cultural and artist circles and meetings of Europe during the 30's, it was pointed as the ideal Mediterranean village. Visiting it, and if possible staying there for a while, was the magic dream that thousands of people of the Old Continent longed to do. It was then when it received the name of "Babel of the Arts". There lived artists of different countries and the native languages mixed with the languages of Marc Chagall, Zügel, Kars, Foujita, Petersen, Brignoni and Masson.

In this crucial moment of the life at Tossa, the museum located in the former house of the Governor was born, inside the walls of the city. Professor Alberto del Castillo, Rafael Benet, painter and art writer, Enrique Casanovas, sculptor and some other artists and intellectuals that were at Tossa, promoted its foundation. This museum would shelter the archaeological collections of Dr. Melé, the village doctor, a man of great culture who had discovered an important Roman village with ruins of the 1st to 4th Centuries. There was also some things to show

*of the medieval population and a considerable show of the artistic pro-
duction made at Tossa, the collection of paintings and sculptures of
the ages between the wars, as it was called, and that was made of
works of prestigious foreign painters, Marc Chagall, Klein, Metzinger,
Kars, Kampf, Zügel, the well-known national works of Hugué, Monjo,
Clará, Creixams, Benet, Bosch, Roger, Sisquella, Togores, Serra,
Domingo, Lola Bech, Colom, Armengol, Canals and several others.
From the 50's the international phenomenon of tourism has invaded
Tossa, thanks to the modern means of transport. The hotels have
been modernised and increased and each year the tourism arrival
increases. Tossa, is, maybe, with some other villages of the Costa
Brava, the one that still keeps a character of beauty and personality
that are its main attractive, despite the continuous transformation. Its
landscape, its holds and beaches, its streets and monuments, its
vegetation, are still of an unbelievable beauty. It still inspires those
who visit it, because as you will see in the images of this book, it is
still the "Flower of the Sea", the beauty of the Costa Brava.*

Vicente Esteban Darder

TOSSA DE MAR

It is the coast sector of the province of Gerona named Costa Brava, for its rugged configuration, in which Tossa de Mar is located. Fishermen village, and once an important Roman harbour that, even today with its medieval walled city, is at the same time one of the most remarkable shows of the remote human presence in the Mediterranean shores and very important centre of international tourism. In order to place it better geographically, we should add that it is located in the region of La Selva so named because, if we go up to the mountains, we will see that the mountains and valleys go from the tops of the Montseny to the sea creating a "jungle" not at all common with a vegetation made of beech trees, oaks and nut trees beyond the hillsides where the weather is, practically, typical of high mountain parts, while the holm oaks forest go down to the sea. In this area, rural tourism is reaching really important occupation levels. This is the meridian sector of the three with which the Costa Brava is divided, this means, the part that goes from

Blanes to Begur and that results from the contact with the sea creating the granite mountains of the Catalonian shores, the Serra de Gavarres, on its way down from 500 m high to the sea. These mountains of Les Gavarres, which may be a good reason to do countless day trips, is a tangible reality in what refers o its climate effects that guards the coast of the area, and thus it guards Tossa of the damages of the northern winds. A protection that together with the advantageous effects of the atmosphere conditions of the Mediterranean Sea, allows Tossa enjoying a temperature exceptionally mild, even during most part of the winter. Another of the attractions Tossa has is its incredible seaside location, facing the bay of the same name, with the privilege of a wide and well protected beach with isles that close it to the east, apart of the surroundings, nearby beaches, rocky cliffs to the east and west really astonishing, of special beauty. Equally, it should be added that the people of this town, as human element, arouses our interest because of their peculiar personality, their undeniable virtues and attachment to former habits and traditions so, to the history and arts that met at Tossa de mar, the traditional taste of being a mainly fisher town adds.

Together with its municipal area, Tossa create a district located to the east of Santa Coloma de Farners, and it belongs to its jurisdiction. The said municipality reaches an extension of 38.18 km^2, with an approximate census of 4.000 inhabitants, this is, more than 100 inhabitants per squared kilometre. The capital village of the municipality has around 3.500 inhabitants, but the changing population of foreigners, just in the tourist season, adds some other thousands. The distance that separates Tossa from Barcelona, for example is of 81 km and 42 from Gerona. Thus, it is only 95 km away of Portbou, in the French frontier. Speaking about the communications, as main asset it has the railway that links the French frontier at Portbou with Barcelona and Tarragona. Although this railway does not have access to most of the seaside villages of the Costa Brava, at Figueres, Flaça and Caldes de Malavella there are several trans-

fer lines that easy the link with several bus lines to the said villages and with Tossa de Mar. Also there are several bus companies that cover the direct route from Gerona and Blanes to Tossa or from Barcelona to Palafrugell, stopping at Tossa; or from Barcelona to Torroella de Montgrí, changing with other lines that take you to Tossa. With private means of transport, as it is logical, access to Tossa is faster using roads and motorways, with excellent highways and simple lines, that run along the Costa Brava and that communicates , not only the villages, but the beaches, the moderns complexes and the holds of the said coast with the main points of the internal part of the region with the frontier with France and the cities of Barcelona and Gerona. Like the rest of the Catalonian coast, Tossa has at reach air transportation by the airports of Barcelona, Girona-Costa Brava and Reus. However, as it is away of the commercial routes or of high traffic, Tossa has an incredibly privileged location, protected and nearly hidden in a corner of beautiful sights and facing the sea. It is a wonderful place to spend time calmly

Roman village of "Ametllers" (4th C.)

and contemplatively, a permanent oasis of well-being, but this does not avoid that, as we have said, it is communicated by road with the rest of the villages of the coast and with the internal region.

HISTORY

Like being some other places of the Mediterranean coast, at Tossa, and its surroundings, traces that revealed the precedents of former inhabitants have been found: Celts, Iberians, Hellenes and Romans. Enter in the days of the historical facts, we found a construction near the police where the present (Vil.la Vitalis) is built. It was a village over really existent in the 1st Century of our time and that was built over a former construction. In agreement with the evident sense found in archaeological diggings, we can estate the visibility was already working on the 2nd Century BC to the 4th Century AD, and over that same village, another one was build because of the needs of increase and improvement of the previous and that should have been finished three centuries after the first. These discovers were done in 1914 by Dr. Ignacio Melé, the doctor of the village, when some diggings took place in the site known as "Els Ametllers", located in the hillside of "Turó d´en Magí".

As some houses were demolished, in what used to be the main square of "Vila Vella", the foundations of some walls of similar construction to that of the Roman village were found by Doctor Melé at "Els Ametllers". This has made us believe that, inside the walled city of the 12th or 13th Century of Vila Vella, there was once, in the era of the Romans another wall system of smaller dimensions. It is thought that the Roman village was occupied until the 7th or 8th Century, date when it was turned into a necropolis. The present look of the wall is due to a reconstruction of that existing in 1387. These defence walls served to protect the city from the pirates' attacks that took place in different times. In 1920 the digs began by Dr. Melé continued under the direction of Professor Schulten. Later, in 1933, they continued under the sponsorship of the Institut d´Estudis Catalans and, later on,

Floor of the Roman village of "Ametllers" of the 4th Century that was part of the former Roman Turissa in the medieval age and the present *Tossa*. As it can be seen, it is a geometrical traditional mosaic.

they were directed by Professor Alberto del Castillo, on behalf of the Museum of Archaeology of Barcelona and the request of the City Hall of Tossa.

The results of all it was the addition to the previous discovering of the oil mill and the storages of a village of the 1st and 2nd Centuries of our time; two series of rooms covered with rich mosaics one of them of the 3rd or 4th Century, is one of the most interesting ever discovered in our country. In it, we see the image and the name of the owner, "Salvus Vital"; the name of the village, "Turissa", and that of the author of the mosaic. Also rests from other rooms were found and a wall of thirty meters long. In, 1934, while the walls, floors and mosaics of the rooms discovered were protected and ordered, new diggings took place that led to the discovering, under the floors before mentioned, to heating by hot air installations, a wonderful swimming pool and some other rooms of the same houses. When mentioning this important works of investigation, the writer Josep Plà, in one of his writings about the history of Tossa, highlights with

Mosaic of the entry to the Roman village of "Ametllers". In the centre we see the image of who used to be the owner of the said village, and the inscription *"Salvo Vitale Felix Turissa-Ex Of Ficina Felices"*, which mean is: *"To Salvus Vital, Felix of Turissa dedicated this mosaic"*. This means, that it gives the name of the owner and of the artist of the work.

detail that the said heating system and swimming pool belong to an era precedent to that of the mosaics of the 3rd and 4th Centuries found on the same place.

Likewise, some coins of the 1st and 2nd Century were picked up. Thus, all these archaeological samples, and other recently found, give us an idea of the importance of the Roman village of "Turissa". In what makes reference to previous times, Alberto del Castillo informs us, when writing in one of his documented and notable studies: "We believe that the area of Tossa could have been occupied by an Iberian population". Later in the same work and speaking about the Roman site of Tossa, he writes: "The location of the village was excellent. In the valley of the mountain over the beach, at about some five hundred meters of the Iberian-Roman village of "Turissa", near the cape of Tossa and on the way to the harbour – he makes reference to the rocky hold of "d'es Codolar" – to the natural routes towards "La Selva", its location was excellent".

As we have already explained, over the ruins of the primitive

Roman village another one was built, result of a higher prosperity and power. We have notices of that until the 8th Century and it is sure that it was destroyed by a fire in a war action. "That is how the history of Turissa ends", says the author of the "Llibre de Tossa", Josep Palau. Then begins that of *"Tursia"*, name of the medieval village that is today called "Vila Vella". This former "Tursia" or medieval Tossa, declared artistic historical monument in 1931, is located on the Guardí mount and, it is still today protected by its walls, provides us with a faithful simple of what were the villages of the feudal age. And these are the famous walled city and defence towers, a work of the 12th and 13th Centuries although some areas have had recovering works, that give to Tossa its singular profile, the unmistakable image know in the whole world as one of the most interesting and enchanting places of the Costa Brava. An image that has been photographed thousands of time and continuous subject of paintings and drawings. In a time, these monumental fortresses counted with five small rounded towers and five bigger ones,

also rounded. Of all of them, there are only kept today: that of the *"Homenaje" o "d´es Codolar"*, that controls the hold – former harbour- of the same name; that of the entry to the city named *"les Hores"*, because there was the public clock of the village in a most recent time to that of the construction, and the *"d´en Joanàs"* that, today still untouched, is the one that arises over the Cape of Tossa. Not so long ago there was one on the hill of the castle, but in 1916, it was demolished to build a modern lighthouse and from where we have one of the most incredible panoramic views of all the shore. We can see from there the ruins of another tower, that of the former dynamite storage. In a hold in the road up, there are ruins of the former "Parish Church" of gothic stile which, like the most recent part of the walls, is dated on the 13th Century. The damages caused in this temple by natural forces and the rage of men are so serious that only a part of the lateral walls and of the apse are still up. As it was useless, it was substituted by the new church that is located in the modern downtown.

The ancient village protected by the walls (12th C.) and by the rocky cliffs that surround it, had as only entry and exit the door next to the "Torre de les Hores", which is still today the natural access to the "Vila Vella". This entry – tells us the remarkable writer of the area Josep Plà – was double, this means, that it was protected by an external revolving door and an internal lifting door. In case of attack the gaps between the two doors was filed with sand sacks so it create an impassable wall.

This only entry gave access, on first term, to the main square in which two other doors had been opened to give access to the inner part of the village. One of them opened to one of the sides of the "del Batlle o Gobernador" street, so called because on the other side of it was the house of the said authority (Casa Falguera – this family was the representative of the abbot of Ripoll, feudal lord of the Village -), detached in the internal part to the "Torre del Homenaje or d´es Codolar". Today, this house holds the Tossa Museum. The other door of the main square gave entry to the village by the street that went under the bridge, called "d'en Riera". Thus, in case that entry was forced through the double door of the wall it was obligatory to pass the two other gates to reach the centre of the city. Facing the danger of the pirates' attacks and of the sea invasion of the enemies, the inhabitants of this coasts, half fishermen half country people, whether they refuge inside their city, what most of them did, whether they locked the city with a defensive system. The people of Tossa chose this second option. This decision was justified by the said circumstance of being surrounded by the rocky hills. The population got known because it offered a safe refuge to travellers and sailors that past by in moments of conflict. Documents of the 10th Century testify that the Earl of Barcelona donated to the Monastery of Ripoll of the city of Tossa that belonged to the bishop and to the city of Gerona. In 966, Berenguer made effective that donation. In the 12th Century, Berenguer 2nd, first and then Berenguer 3rd, confirmed it.

It is since then when Tossa appears in the documents with the name of "Castrum de Tursia" (Castle of Tursia). In virtue of determined dispositions of the abbot of Ripoll, the village later acquired several privileged and, in 1359, it counted with the following hierarchy: a "Castila", person in charge of directing the defence of the fortresses; a "Batlle" or governor of the jurisdiction to administer justice and a "Batlle de Sac" dedicated to the collection of the feudal taxes. The administration was done by three judges, a "Clavari" or treasurer and the Council constituted by twenty one people of the village, chosen at random between all the stages of the population. It is known that, when there was a situation difficult to solve, it was submitted to the deliberation and resolution of the General Council constituted by the heads of the families of Tossa. In the 12th Century we see that the said charges belonged to an assembly of fifty people. As patrimony free of all feudal charge, the king Jaime the second gave to Odón de Montcada, amongst other things several castles, the fortress of Tossa, which cause conflicts with the monks of Ripoll; this conflict was won by the monks who kept the ownership of the fortress and village of Tossa. It is not until the 14th Century when, with some conditions, the Monastery of Ripoll gave the jurisdictional major of Tossa to several leaders of the families. This is who we know that the Soler, Riera, Vern, Folguera and other families with members still alive carried out this charges. In agreement with the information provided by the historian José Soler de Morell, reporter of every thing that happened, we know that, from the date of the concessions, Tossa entered in the system of the general administration following, thus, the vicissitudes of the rest of the villages of the country. On the other side, reducing the danger of the pirates in the Mediterranean, after the Battle of Lepanto, the people who, like those of Tossa, lived in the shores of the sea, felt safer and began to get used to live outside the walled city. "We believe that it is not risky to think, write Josep Palau- that, at the beginning of the 17th Century, already existed a remarkable number of houses outside the former perimeter and of this expansion the

present Tossa was born".

The watch towers contributed to provide more safety to the inhabitants who, in that period, Felipe 2nd order to build along the Mediterranean coast and which local testimony is "Torre dels Moros" or "Can Magí".

Another important point in this urban development was the chapel of "Verge dels Socors" which construction was paid by Antoni Caixa as ex-voto to the said Virgin for saving him from drowning. The fishermen and traders of the area were very devoted to this Virgin, so the chapel became a very important meeting point. Nowadays, it is where the procession of "Pelegrí de Tossa" ends when it comes backs from Santa Coloma de Farners.

To this time also belongs the construction of the "Hospital de Sant Miquel" founded, in 1765, by Tomás Vidal. It has a central square and a chapel attached of baroque style. It is a perfect state of conservation because it was restored and, today, it is the siege of the House of Culture of the city.

Separated form the guard of the Monastery of Ripoll, Tossa acquires a higher importance in the life of the region. Ruled by the Municipal Council, this, in 1755 makes an agreement to build a new temple because the former was too small in relation to the increase in the population outside the walls of the city and also because it was very damaged by the air and the lack of conservation and was about to become a ruin. This is how the temple, which ruins can still be seen on the way to the light house, was abandoned, and in 1777, the new Church of Sant Vicenç was finished that is now in the centre of the present city of Tossa. To be true, even today is big enough for the population of Tossa.

But there are other reason, several others, that have made of Tossa "the pearl and pride of the Costa Brava", as it was called in the verses of Joan Oliver and Joan Guarro. Some time before, and especially in the Roman age, Tossa had been an important harbour. From the Middle Age to the end of the 18th Century, it kept and active commerce of cabotage with other Mediterranean populations. The optimal position of its economy was reinforced when intensifying its fishing and agriculture activity. On the other side, Tossa was one of the villages that took more advantage of the prosperous national commerce in the 18th and 19th Centuries. However, this chapter of Tossa's history ends in the 20th Century. The cabotage commerce and the cork industries have disappeared and Tossa had economic problems and the treat of misery begins to be seen as a real problem. A lot of people left the city, most of them to travel to America. From 1990 inhabitants in 1860 it passed to 1339 in 1950. But, some years later, Tossa recovers from that collapse because of an unpredicted and exceptional phenomenon: international tourism. With the arrival of more and more people from all the parts of the world, the former fishermen village has transformed, modernised and increase completely.

TOSSA DE MAR TODAY

It is a difficult task to describe the surroundings of Tossa de Mar because its incredible beauty goes beyond what the foreigner could have imagine before visiting it.

House of one, two or more floors, big buildings with a lot of houses, hotels, residences, bars, pubs, shops and other premises, normal in the most important tourism centres of the country, have found their place at Tossa in an incredible way during

these last years. The massive flux of foreigners, to which Tossa owes its prosperous change, is a consequence of the great prestige acquired by the Costa Brava as a whole. But it is also true that all the places that soon contributed to the said prestige, or that spread it, Tossa was, without any doubt, of the first to achieve an international name. It is due, maybe, to a singular fact, that some of the painters and writers of the country, together with foreign artists and intellectuals, coincide in spending at the village some seasons, especially between 1932 and 1939 and after World War One.

As we have already said, Tossa was called the "Babel of the Arts" because those artists did not follow a determined trend (all of them belonging to avant-guard trends of the age; impressionism, cube expressionism and other art trends) but all of them choose Tossa to spend some time there because of the beauty of the landscape. We have said that it is a singular fact and we should add, that it was fully justified by the beauties and attractive of the village and its surroundings that they all loved

Es Codolar

and included in some of their work. This is how Josep Plà explains this new chapter in the history of Tossa: "It was really remarkable the amount of foreign tourism that concentrated at Tossa. This trend also had a special nuance: that of being made of painters, sculptors and men of arts. The Catalonian affluence mixed with the foreigner. Tossa became known in all the European literature coffee shops and became a curious centre. The beach, at the time of the bath, the foreign hotels, the "Café d'en Biel", the taverns, became the unmistakable stamp of the artist cosmopolitism".

Of this period are the improvements made at "Vila Vella", the creation of the Municipal Museum inaugurated in 1935 that can be considered the fist contemporary art museum in Spain. As we have already said, this museum locates inside the walled city, in the 14th Century building that was formerly inhabited by the governor of the city or "Batlle del Sac" and that was by the "Torre d´es Codolar". There we can enjoy important archaeological collections that witness the presence of the inhabitants of the area from the Palaeolithic, sculpture, painting and worked glass, Roman mosaics, found in the Roman village of "Els Ametllers" of the 4th and 5th Centuries, discovered by Dr. Ignasi Melé in 1914, the paintings of important foreign artists like Marc Chagall, André Masson, Olga Sacharof, André Klein and the Catalonian Joaquín Sunyer, Rafael Benet, Pere Créixams, Lola Bech, Emili Armengol. All these artists left their trace of the great natural beauty of Tossa de Mar.

The idea of the creation of the museum is due, amongst other, to the artists that spent some time at Tossa and decided to leave documents of the image of the town in some of their works. The most representative were the archaeologist Ignacio del Castillo, who was the first director, and the Catalonian painters Benet and Créixams, the sculptor Casanovas and the painters Lola Bech and George Kars, amongst others.

Tossa is at our reach and enjoyment. It is located where Costa Brava is more generous with its natural gifts. To the magic of its beaches and holds, rocks, cliffs and escapes to the sea, it

offers, inside, the most attractive essences of the fields. To the soft or rough configuration of the mountains, the analogue diversity of forests, valleys and agriculture lands mix up. Guarded by the "Paseo del Mar", with is beautiful terraces shown in their canvas by some of the famous painters that visited the city, we find the beaches: *"Platja Gran"*, in the centre of the town, a wide beach that has nearly all the services we may need to have a excellent day at the beach: bars, restaurants, parking, toilet areas, docks for tourism ships, cruises, boats with glass floor, deckchair rental, umbrellas, skates, etc. it was awarded with the "Blue Flag" by the European Union for the quality of its services and its clean water; *"Platja del Reig"* to which we can arrive walking because it is just some minutes away of the city centre, small and quite; *"Mar Menuda"*, also some minutes away of the city and its "Blue Flag". If has big grain sand and, as Platja Gran, nearly all the services with dock, tourism cruise, and also bars, restaurants, services, toilets, first aid services, etc.

If we head to the east, to Sant Feliu de Guíxols, we should that

The beautiful and protected Bona hold, it has this name because it is one of the safest places for the boat, no matter what the weather conditions are.

The wonderful beach of Pola, that together with Cona is a part of the same beach, divided by a small sand tongue.

the road the links this city with Tossa – 15 km – and that is now of the most beautiful of the country. Hill road, almost heading over the sea, it slides through the country and then it reaches heights of more than a hundred metres. Changing, although always amazing and astonishing are the landscape views that may be seen on both sides of the road and that lead to *"Serrat dels Moltons"*, *"Puig de l´Agulla"*, *"Mare de Deu de Gràcia"*, etc. When going down facing the sea we find enchanted corners like *"cala Sant Jaume"*, one kilometre away from Tossa, a very small beach with rolling stones and of very difficult access because it is located between cliffs. You can access to it with a boat, and this difficulty is compensated by the beauty of the landscape. *"Cala Bona"* at about 3 km away from Tossa, is a small beach which look is one of the places at Costa Brava where the trees nearly touch the sea. *"Cala Pola"* which access is by road crossing a camping in the area, is a beach of big grain sand and it has a dock for cruises and other services. *"Platja Giverola"* at about five Km of the city is a wide beach with a lot of services.

You arrive to *"Cala Futadera"*, by some stairs that lead to the beach from the parking. It is a sandy beach where we should highlight its clean waters and the depth of the same; a very quiet area with surprising colours, recommended for those who love calms and nature. *"Cala Salions"*, – de "Sant Lionç" – a wide beach of big grain that has most of the services.

If you follow the coast on board of a boat, close to the shore, when possible, there are some more beaches and holds off incredible beauty like those that are close to "Mar Menuda" and "Bandera de Ses Dones", "l´Illa de Sa Palma" and, a little bit away, "Punta de la Bruma", "l´Infern en Caixa", the caves of "l´Esclafada y "El Berganti", "Cap Petiné" and some other enchanting places caused by the erosion of the sea that has change the landscape making it unbelievably beautiful until we arrive to Sant Feliu de Guíxols. It is, without any doubt, one of the most impressive and characteristic places of Costa Brava. We should say that the trip is also incredible if we do the same

Cala Pola towards the interior and thus, showing the landscape of the area.

Two views of Giverola which, as the other beaches and holds of the coast from Tossa to Sant Feliu de Guíxols, has contributed to the world' prestige of Costa Brava.

but heading the opposite direction to Lloret de Mar. This side is more flat, with beaches and holds that seem wider. However, the beauty, enchantment and paradise peace are as easy to find as in the other trip we have mentioned of the Costa Brava.

There is a road that goes at the back of "Vila Vella" to "Turó d´en Magí" and that lets us admire the match at bird's view of "Es Codolar", the former harbour. Later, we will head up until reaching the highest point at "Els Cards"- 116 m high -, where we discover an incredible view in it widest sense. If we are there on a sunny day, we will be able to sea the coast from "Cap de Sant Sebastià" at Palafrugell, to the mountain of "Montjuïc", in Barcelona. At one side, the vast extension of the blue Mediterranean Sea that touches the horizon, on the other, the wonderful contrast of the rocks, the golden beaches, the vegetation that dresses the mountains... If we want to have different views, it is worth going up to the top of "Coll de Canyelles" or to any other of the pinnacles of this line.

When doing this trip from the coast to Lloret de Mar, there are some wonders that are waiting for us, here resumed in a simple enumeration of their names and some short comments: *"Platja d´es Codolar"*, small and calm, at the feet of the walls of Vila Vella, you can get there walking and there are bars, services, showers, etc. *"Cala Moltó"*, *"Punta dels Cards"*, *"Roca del Moro"*, *"Cala Llevadó"*, *"Cala de´n Carlos"*, *"Cala des Rajols"*, *"Sa Boquera"*, *"Platges de Llorell"* at about 3.5 km of Lloret that unites a lot of services and the possibility of practicing several water sports. *"Porto Pi"* and *"Cala Morisca"*, Tossa's last beach, at about 5 km from the city, and one of the last virgin beaches of the Costa Brava. And so on if we have enough time to visit the surroundings of Lloret de Mar, always adding new moments of wonder and surprise.

If we do not have a boat, we recommend doing the sea trips from the beach of Tossa as there are companies specialising in this activity with bigger boats with trips that take you from Calella to Platja d' Aro with stops at Pineda, Santa Susanna, Malgrat, Blanes, Lloret, Sant Feliu de Guíxols and Platja d´Aro.

Cala Giverola

Cala Salions.

Some of these boats have glass floors so you could admire the sea that for some people is an incredible experience.

About the trips to the inner part of the region we would like to add two more. One of them can be divided into several trips. It is leaving Tossa by road to Llagostera and then turning right, after five minutes of walk, to head to "Molí Lluny"; then you take "Camí dels Enamorats", to arrive to the forest of "Can Samada". At kilometre five of this same road, there is a walk that leads to the "Ermita de Sant Benet", an interesting place for those in love with natural beauties.

Another interesting point is "Parque de Sa Riera", located at less than a kilometre away of the city; it is an interesting city park in which we could take a relaxing walk and enjoy watching its lake, natural reserve of different fishes, plants and birds species.

You should also visit the area of Macizo de Cadiretes, a natural reserve that includes Tossa with the purpose of visiting "Puig de les Cadiretes" of 525 m high and also the "Santuari de Sant

Landscape view of the sector of Costa Brava from Tossa to Sant Feliu de Guíxols; the modern and spacious buildings of the back part are cala Salions.

The wonderful Playa de Santa María de Llorell, seen from Punta de Sa Boquera. It goes along the coast between Tossa and Lloret.

Grau" that, in the 60's, was turned into a hotel. Nowadays, it is abandoned and there is a legend about it saying the Sant Grau d´Aurillac lived there during the 9th Century. In 1200, Queen Marie of Montpellier, mother of Jaime I el Conquistador, found some relics of the said Saint for the sanctuary.

All the roads we have to walk, as well as the tops to where they lead, justify the two hours and a half walk. "La Palanca d´en Martí", "Mas Sans", "Sant Grau", "Cal Federal" y "Valls de Rocs" are, the milestones that mark the most interesting paths. With the photographs and foot notes that accompany our text, we complete the information that we have tried to provide the reader about Tossa, "the flower of the Sea", as it is name in some song about the patron saint.

VISITS AND DAY TRIPS

It privileged situation makes Tossa de Mar the centre of inte-resting day trips, both by land or by sea, having the possibility of choosing several interesting tourism point spread throughout

Santa María de Llorell

The hold of Llevadó, very well protected by the cliffs that made it. It is between Roca del Moro and Punta de Sa Boquera.

Catalonia. We recommend the visits to: **Barcelona**, capital in which, only from the architectural point of view, we could reconstruct more than twenty centuries of history, with Roman art collections unique in the world, that we can visit at "Museu Nacional d´Art de Catalunya". In this cultural offer, we should also highlight the "Museu d´Art Contemporani", "the Museu Picasso" a privilege of Barcelona, or the "Fundaciones Joan Miró or Thyssen". The Gothic Neighbourhood, incredible for its dimensions, and where we could find different buildings to visit like the cathedral, the City Hall that has a neoclassic façade of 1847 or the Palau de la Generalitat with the Yard of the Orange Trees and the Renaissance art façade of the 16th Century. The biggest and most expressive works of the surprising genius of the architect Antonio Gaudí, like the famous building of "La Pedrera", the "La Casa Batlló" and above them all, the majestic temple of "La Sagrada Família". There are other places worth visiting like the zoo, one of the most appreciated in the world; el Museo Marítimo, the Tibidabo, with an excellent fun fair; the

Colón. Sagrada Familia y Casa Milà (La Pedrera) by Antoni Gaudí.

Montserrat

Empúries

El "Port Olímpic"; the "Maremágnum" where the Imax cinema and the "Aquarium" are located etc., and so we could name thousands of places worth visiting. There are some other cities we would like to recommend for their history and beauty, that are:

Montserrat, about 55 Km. away from Barcelona, the sacred mountain of Catalonia, an a wonder of the nature thanks to its attractive geological form, it could also be said that you can visit the Monastery of de Santa Maria, where the Virgin of Montserrat "La Moreneta" is worshiped and the Art Museum with works from Prehistory to our days that include Picasso and Dali. This monastery, some years, has had more than a million visitors.

Banyoles, and its lake, declared by the State in 1951, "Picturesque Landscape", being very attractive to rent a boat in this lake where several water sports like together. This city was one of the Olympic venues in the Games celebrated in 1992.

Gerona, which ancient part is one of the great monumental cities of Spain, with important Gothic and Romanic monuments,

Banyoles

highlighting the Catedral, covered by only one gothic arch of 23 m high that is the highest in the world. The "Banys àrabs" of the 12th Century.

Empúries, with ruins of a former Greek city, located at the Roses gulf that tells us stories of its glorious past.

And so we could name thousands of interesting places like Pals, Besalú, Cadaqués, Figueres, etc., of which you could find enough information at the Tourism Offices of Tossa.

GASTRONOMY, FOLKLORE AND FEASTS

At Tossa de Mar and its surroundings meet the traditional Mediterranean fishermen cooking with that of the mountains so it enjoys an excellent and well deserved gastronomic name. Of the first one we should highlight the fish, seafood and mussels dishes like *"suquet de peix"*, a dish with o fan excellent take in which fried garlic and tomato increase the taste of the fishes that have just been caught and cooked with some potatoes, *"la zarzuela"* a little bit more sophisticated than "suquet", the *"fri-*

tura de pescado" or, *mejillones a la marinera"*, etc. Equally, we can prepare these fishes and seafood cooked in an oven thanks to its quality and the extraordinary taste that they keep if we cook them this was.

We should also highlight the mountains typical cuisine, with vegetables of the north part of the region, with excellent vegetables, fruits, mushrooms (in the season), as well as its excellent meat, etc. We are going to give you names of the most popular dishes: *"escalivada"* (roasted vegetables), *"caracoles con picada"*, *"habas a la catalana"*, *"conejo con nabos o con caracoles"*, *"escudella i carn d´olla a la catalana"*, *"pies de cerdo con guisantes y piñones"*, etc.

There are also some traditional dishes that combine sea products with those of the mountain like "lobster with escargots" or "chicken or rabbit with lobster or crayfish" and "sepia with meat balls", etc.

There we can taste too wonderful fruits like watermelons, melons, strawberries, etc., that during the summer they become

the main ingredients of tasty ice-creams, sorbets and desserts. A typical product of the area is honey with a deserved reputation thanks to its quality.

We could still name more stews and dishes both of the traditional cuisines and of the modern and international cuisine, but we prefer that you discover them at the restaurants of Tossa de Mar, from the most exquisite to the cheapest but all of them a mark of the quality of the products.

Speaking about the folklore, the sardana is the popular dance of Catalonia which exact nature is unknown although it seems that it has its origin in the reminiscences of an ancient Greek dance. It was Joan Maragall who made it popular in a poem that for a lot of people is a symbolic representation of the ideal of the Catalonian people. Pep Ventura, musician and son of Figueres, with his compositions and mixes, contributed to its spreading. In this dance anyone who feels like can take part as he would be included in one of the circles that, with the sounds

of music, are created. The sounds are very special because of the instruments they use and the dances dance with their hands together as a symbol of union.

The feasts and events that take place at Tossa de Mar during the year are several. We can highlight the "Fiesta Mayor d´Hivern -winter- de Sant Vicenç" and "Fiesta Mayor d´Estiu –summer- de Sant Pere". That of spring (de St.Vicenç) is celebrated at the end of the month of January (22nd) and they dance sardanas, they have concerts and shows for children. This feast is preceded by the procession of "Pelegrí de Tossa" that is celebrated the day before at the monastery of Santa Coloma de Farners. The second "Fiesta Mayor" (that of St. Pere) is celebrated at the end of the month of June (29th) and we will also enjoy the typical dances, concerts, shows for children, fireworks, etc. During the month of June, and before the "Fiesta Mayor" there are other feasts: on 5th there is a concert "d´havaneres" and a "cremat popular", the 6th is the

"Fishermen day" with a sardine barbecue and dancing of sardanas, on 10th it is the Corpus Christi procession with flower carpets; on 2nd July it is the traditional "Toquen a córrer, ses nou sardanes". During the month of August there is an International Music Festival, a fair of drawing and paintings and the International Painting Award of Tossa de Mar; during the second half of August the International Day of Tourism is celebrated. And so we could speak about different events but the tourist can have more information at their hotel reception and at the Tourism Office of those that are going to take place while they are there.

At last, and as ending comment, it could be thought that, nearly always, the publications of tourism books tends to exaggerate the beauty of the places it describes, so the tourist who is not very well informed may have the thought that the world is full of wonderful places, with cheap hotels, excellent climates and always friendly places.

Monument to Minerva.

This short guide about Tossa de Mar, and its surroundings, has tried not to do that. The area has thousand of attractive places both for their history and for it surroundings, as it is shown in the pictures that illustrate it. About the character of its people, we leave it to de tourist to discover their humble and welcoming character. This is a geographical, historical and, in away, vital vision of the city of Tossa de Mar and its surroundings. If we have manage to make it interesting for you to visit the city or if we have achieved that this guide serves as souvenir of the days spent in the city, we would have achieved our purpose.

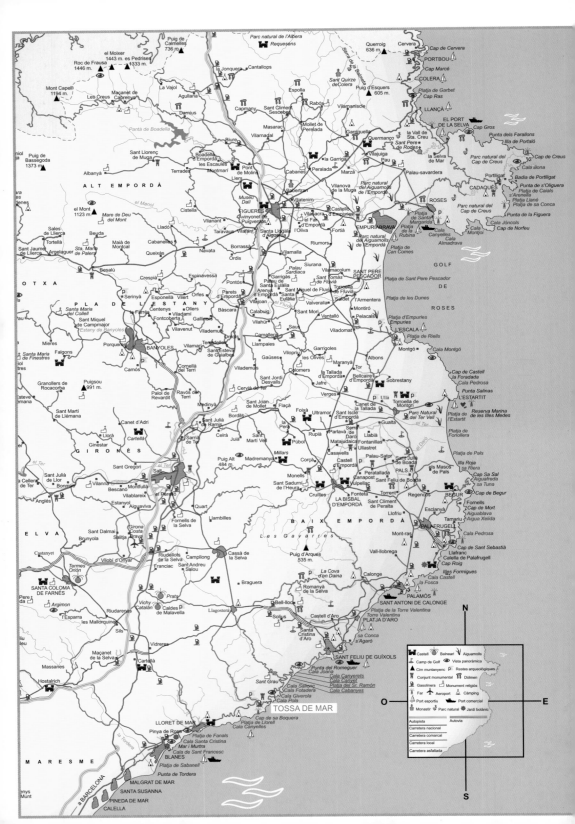